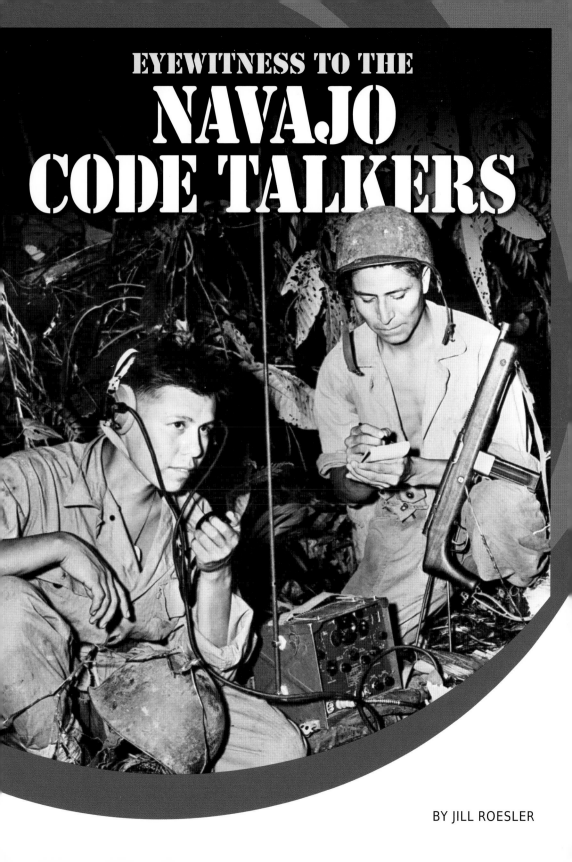

EYEWITNESS TO THE
NAVAJO
CODE TALKERS

BY JILL ROESLER

Published by The Child's World®
1980 Lookout Drive • Mankato, MN 56003-1705
800-599-READ • www.childsworld.com

Acknowledgments
The Child's World®: Mary Berendes, Publishing Director
Red Line Editorial: Design, editorial direction, and production
Photographs ©: Corbis, cover, 1, 14; Everett Historical/Shutterstock Images, 4, 16, 20;
Bettmann/Corbis, 6, 12, 18; Hulton-Deutsch Collection/Corbis, 9; Russell Lee/Library
of Congress, 10; AP Images, 23; U.S. Marine Corps/Library of Congress, 24; Ron
Edmonds/AP Images, 27; Mark Skalny/Shutterstock Images, 29

ISBN 9781634074186

LCCN 2015946226

Printed in the United States of America
Mankato, MN
December, 2015
PA02281

ABOUT THE AUTHOR

Jill Roesler is from southern Minnesota. In addition to writing children's
books, she writes for several newspapers. Her favorite subject to research
and write about is history. In her free time, Roesler enjoys reading, traveling,
and gardening.

TABLE OF
CONTENTS

Chapter 1

A SECRET CODE

It was a sunny Sunday afternoon in 1941. A group of boys were gathered together for a meal. They attended Ganado Mission School in Arizona. The students were Native Americans. They were all members of the Navajo tribe. At home, they spoke the Navajo language. But at school, they spoke English.

Suddenly, a friend sprinted over to them. He had just heard some alarming news. "The United States has been attacked," the student gasped. "We're in a war!"[1]

Two years earlier, World War II had begun in Europe. The war was between the Allies and the Axis Powers. The Allies included Britain, France, and Canada. The Axis Powers included Germany, Italy, and Japan. The United States supported the Allies. But many U.S. leaders and citizens did not want to fight in the war. Instead, they gave money and weapons to help the Allies.

All of that changed on Sunday, December 7, 1941. Japanese forces attacked Pearl Harbor, a U.S. Navy base in Hawaii. Soon, the United States would officially declare war on Japan.

Keith Little, one of the Ganado students, was angry about the surprise attack. He was proud of his country. Little wanted to help defend it. Soon after he heard about the attack, Little saw a poster for the United States Marine Corps (USMC). As soon as he could, he **enlisted**.

Little attended USMC training in San Diego, California. The exercises were often difficult. But Little was determined to succeed. One day, he noticed a drill instructor looking at him. The instructor asked, "By any chance are you a Navajo?"

"Yes, sir," Little replied.[2] The instructor told him about a new program. The USMC was training Navajo Marines to send messages. They would use a secret code based on the Navajo language.

For years, Little had been forbidden from speaking Navajo. His teachers at Ganado Mission School wanted him to speak English instead. Suddenly, Little had the chance to use his native language. His ability to understand both English and Navajo would help the military communicate secret plans.

"When I went into the Marine Corps . . . I knew nothing about the Navajo code. It was really astonishing to me to get to Camp Pendleton and there were a bunch of Navajos there, and they were working with a Navajo code."

—Keith Little[3]

During the war, spies were everywhere. Government organizations used posters to warn Americans. "The enemy is listening," said one. "He wants to know what you know."[4] Both the Axis Powers and the Allies used codes to send secret information. Often, they **intercepted** messages. Secret agents

◀ In a 1940s classroom, a teacher helped Navajo children learn English.

would try to crack the enemy's code. To keep the military plans secret, the code needed to be strong and difficult.

Soon, a group of Navajo Marines would begin sending military messages. They would use their language to create a secret code.

Chapter 2

THE FIRST CODE TALKERS

The U.S. military had used a Native American language for secret communications before. During World War I, members of the Choctaw tribe worked as "code talkers." They sent U.S. Army messages in their native language.

Enemy countries intercepted some of the messages. But the Choctaw language puzzled them. They could not **decode** the messages. After the war, some countries sent agents to the United States. The agents studied the Choctaw language. They wanted to be prepared for future wars.

When World War II began, military officials considered using the Choctaw language in secret messages again. But they knew that some enemy agents had learned to read Choctaw. Using the language was too risky. An army engineer named Philip Johnston had an idea.

Johnston grew up in Arizona in the early 1900s. His father, a preacher, worked on a local Navajo **reservation**. At first, Johnston could not understand any Navajo words. To Johnston, the words sounded unusual. The language was very difficult to learn. For many years, it had no written form. Few non-Navajos could speak the language. Johnston struggled to communicate with others. But over time, he learned to speak Navajo.

Years later, Johnston learned about the Choctaw code talkers. He remembered how difficult it was to learn the Navajo language. Could Navajo be used to create a code?

▲ A Navajo mother and daughter tended crops on a Navajo reservation in 1939.

After the attack on Pearl Harbor, Johnston met with Lieutenant Colonel James Jones. He told Jones about the Navajo language. This language, he thought, could help U.S. forces send "a message that no enemy could possibly understand."[5]

At first, Jones was doubtful. What if German and Japanese agents learned the Navajo language? Then they would be able to decode the messages. But Johnston had a different idea. "My plan is not to use **translations** of an Indian language, but to build up a code of Indian words," he said.[6]

The lieutenant colonel thought about the idea. Johnston decided to try speaking in the Navajo language. He wanted to show Jones how difficult it was for many people to understand the language. Jones stared at him in amazement. The Navajo language sounded like nothing he had heard before. "Mr. Johnston," he said, "you may have something there!"[7]

Jones wanted to meet with Navajo men. So Johnston began a search. For two weeks, he found Navajos who could become code talkers. The men had to speak both English and Navajo. They would need to switch quickly between the two languages.

In February 1942, Johnston and four Navajo men met with Jones. The lieutenant colonel handed a piece of paper to Johnston. "Here are six typical messages," he said. "See what your men can do with them. Report to me in an hour."[8]

The Navajo men had one hour to create a simple code using Navajo words. Then they had to translate the messages into the Navajo code and back into English. Major General Clayton Vogel reviewed the results. "These are excellent translations," he said. "There's no doubt in my mind that Navajo words could be used for code purposes."[9]

The USMC agreed to try out the Navajo code talker project. On May 5, 1942, 29 men began working on the first Navajo code.

Chapter 3

BUILDING THE CODE

I n May 1942, the new Navajo Marines reported to Camp Elliott in California. These Marines became known as the "Original 29." The men met secretly in a classroom. They had to work quickly. The Marines had just two months to develop a code. Sometimes, the men argued. "They put us all in a room to work it out," said Chester Nez. "It seemed impossible, because even among ourselves, we didn't agree on all the right Navajo words."[10]

Day and night, armed guards patrolled the camp. **Escorts** followed the code talkers everywhere. The code talkers could not discuss their work with their families. Even some senior USMC officers did not know about it. The Marines were determined to keep the code a secret.

Eventually, the code talkers succeeded. They created a code of 211 words. Many military words did not exist in the Navajo language. For example, there was no Navajo word for *fighter plane*. Instead, the code talkers used *da-he-tih-hi*. This word means "hummingbird" in Navajo. The Navajo word for *turtle* was used for *tank*. Code talkers also chose words for each letter of the alphabet. That way, they could use the code to spell out words.

"It was my country that was attacked by the Japanese. I had no choice. . . . I had to join the Marines. I had to be a warrior."

—*Chester Nez, a Navajo code talker*[11]

▲ **The Navajo language did not have words for many military vehicles, including tanks.**

Code talkers had to memorize each of the original 211 Navajo words. They could not rely on written records. "Those of us who . . . learned the code couldn't take notes out of the classroom," said Peter MacDonald.[12] Enemy spies might find the notes. The spies could use them to crack the code.

While the men memorized the code, they also learned about the special equipment that they would use. Code talkers would communicate with each other by radio. Most had little experience with this technology. However, they learned quickly. Code talkers practiced taking apart their radios and putting them back together. They tested sending coded messages and translating them.

USMC project leaders were pleased with the code talkers' work. But they needed more code talkers. Quickly, the Original 29 began to train new **recruits**. Learning the code was not easy. The Original 29 printed a dictionary to help new code talkers. The dictionary could be used in the classroom only. The code talkers did not want it to fall into enemy hands.

Soon, the Original 29 had trained nearly 200 additional code talkers. It was time to test the code in action. In fall 1942, the first code talkers were sent to the battlefields.

Chapter 4

ON THE BATTLEFIELDS

I n 1942, U.S. Marines were fighting Japanese forces. Battles occurred mostly on islands in the Pacific. On August 7, 1942, a battle began on the island of Guadalcanal.

The Marines needed people to pass messages from one unit to another. These messages needed to be in code. That way, Japanese officers would not learn about U.S. plans. On November 4, the first group of

Navajo code talkers arrived. Code talkers would be assigned to different combat units. They would send messages over the radio from one unit to another.

"A **runner** approached, handing me a message written in English," wrote Chester Nez. "It was my first battlefield transmission in Navajo code. I'll never forget it."[13] The message warned of Japanese machine guns nearby. It directed Marines to destroy the guns.

Nez held the radio microphone and repeated the warning in Navajo code. Soon, another code talker received the message. Quickly, he translated the message into English. Then he reported it to troops around him. "Suddenly, just after my message was received, the Japanese guns exploded," wrote Nez.[14] U.S. forces had destroyed them. Nez felt a sense of pride and excitement.

The code talkers were successfully sharing information. But their messages confused some other Marines. These Marines did not know what the Navajo language sounded like. They thought that the language they were hearing was Japanese.

19

"The radio was buzzing, the telephone was ringing," said one code talker.[15] Many Marines were afraid that Japanese forces had taken control of U.S. communications.

Word of the problems reached Lieutenant Colonel Jones. At first, he wanted to send the Navajo Marines back to camp. But then Jones proposed a test for the code talkers. If they passed the test, the code talkers could stay. Jones wanted to see if they could decode a message faster than he could. Both Jones and a code talker sent coded messages to another unit. Each man received an answer. Whoever could decode the answer first would win the challenge.

"How long will it take you?" the colonel asked. "Two hours?"

"Two hours? I can get [it] ready in two minutes," the code talker said.[16] Less than five minutes later, he had decoded the message. The lieutenant colonel had hardly begun. The code talkers would stay.

At the time, there were six Marine divisions in the Pacific. Officers assigned a group of Navajo communicators to each division. During battles, the Navajo Marines often worked behind enemy lines. They had to send and decode military messages very quickly. That was not a problem for the code talkers. They

◀ **Starting in 1942, code talkers traveled with groups of Marines on Pacific islands.**

21

> "Sometimes we had to crawl, had to run. . . . But there was no problem. We transmitted our messages under any and all conditions."
>
> *—Navajo code talker[17]*

cut old encoding and decoding times in half. In 20 seconds, a code talker could put a short message into code, **transmit** it, and translate the response into English.

The Navajo code was fast and nearly error-free. More importantly, it stayed top secret. The enemy was unable to break it. Code talkers added more words to the code. By fall 1942, there were more than 410 words. The code continued to grow. So did the Marines' need for Navajo recruits.

The USMC rushed to train more code talkers. Each had to complete eight weeks of communications training at Camp Pendleton in California. By April 1943, 200 more recruits had completed their training. By the end of the war, about 400 code talkers were sending and receiving messages.

New code talkers completed their training at Camp Pendleton ▶ in California.

Chapter 5

KEEPING SECRETS

The code talkers had proven their skills. But their work was only beginning. Like all Marines, they braved dangers in the Pacific. They worked long hours in sweltering heat, sometimes without food or water. Some were injured or killed in battle. But the code talkers took great pride in their work.

"Our language was a weapon," said code talker Thomas Begay. "That's how I saw it. We have all kinds of battle scars."[18]

One key event was the Battle of Iwo Jima. A tiny volcanic island in the Pacific, Iwo Jima was covered in ash. The terrain was difficult for fighting. Troops struggled to advance among steep hills and boulders. But the small island was close to Japan. Capturing the island would help U.S. forces attack Japanese cities. Warplanes could refuel on the island.

U.S. Marines landed on Iwo Jima on February 19, 1945. At first, they were startled by the stillness of the island. They saw only a few Japanese troops. Perhaps taking the island would be easy. But then the Marines made an alarming discovery. The Japanese military had built underground tunnels throughout the island. Soon, they began making surprise attacks from the tunnels. Despite a heavy exchange of fire, some U.S. troops never even saw a Japanese soldier.

American Marines searched the scorched earth for tunnels and Japanese weapons. Marines and navy men fired into the tunnels, but often failed to hit their targets. Code talker Chester Nez remembered preparing for the battle. He heard a lieutenant say that the enemy would be almost impossible to beat.

Code talkers shared information about the tunnels with different units. That way, they could prevent surprise attacks. For the first two days of the battle, six code talkers worked without sleep. They sent 800 messages in the first 48 hours.

The code talkers risked their lives to send messages during the battle. "We were out on the **front line**," said Sam Billison. "That's where the messages have to come from."[19]

The battle was hard-fought. For weeks, Marines threw grenades and shot machine guns into the tunnels. Thousands of American soldiers were killed or wounded. But Japan suffered even heavier losses. On March 26, 1945, American forces declared victory. The battle had lasted for 36 long days. The code talkers helped the United States win the battle. Major Howard Connor said, "Were it not for the Navajos, the Marines would never have taken Iwo Jima."[20]

Less than two months later, Germany surrendered to the Allies. The war in the Pacific, where the code talkers worked, raged on. While Allied forces gained ground, Japan was reluctant to surrender. Finally, in August 1945, Japanese forces surrendered to the Allies. They never cracked the Navajo code.

The code talkers returned home. But the change was difficult. Many code talkers were deeply proud of their work. But they

▲ President George W. Bush congratulated code talker John Brown on his Congressional Gold Medal.

could not talk about their war service. They still had to keep the code secret. The military might want to use the code again.

Soon, code talkers had a chance to return to the battlefields. In June 1950, the United States entered the Korean War. The U.S. Marine Corps again used code talkers to send and receive messages. In 1965, the code was used for the Vietnam War. Many World War II code talkers volunteered.

> "Today America honors 29 Native Americans. . . . In war, using their native language, they relayed secret messages that turned the course of battle. At home, they carried for decades the secret of their own heroism."
>
> —*President George W. Bush, presenting the Original 29 code talkers with medals*[21]

In 1968, the Navajo code was finally made public. By then, the military could use computer programs to build complicated codes. They did not need the code talkers any longer. For the first time, Navajo code talkers could talk openly about their service. Still, few people knew about their brave deeds. For years, the code talkers did not receive much recognition.

Slowly, that began to change. Some code talkers spoke publicly about their war experiences. Historians wrote about how the code talkers helped the U.S. war effort. In 2001, the Original 29 code talkers received the Congressional Gold Medal. It was 59 years after the code was created. "I often thought we'd never get recognized," said Chester Nez. "This is one special occasion for us."[22]

Former code talker Keith Little attended an event for veterans ▶ in 2008.

GLOSSARY

decode (de-KOHD): To decode a secret message is to change it into its original language. During wartime, both sides tried to decode the enemy's messages.

enlisted (en-LIST-ed): A person who has enlisted in a group has joined the group. Some Navajos enlisted in the U.S. Marine Corps.

escorts (ES-kawrts): Escorts are guards or protectors. Often, escorts guided code talkers around the camp.

front line (FRUHNT LEYN): People on the front line are the first people to go into battle. Fighters on the front line faced many dangers.

intercepted (in-ter-SEP-ted): When a message is intercepted, it is taken or seized. Japanese forces intercepted some U.S. military messages.

recruits (ri-KROOTZ): Recruits are new members of a military force. More experienced code talkers trained the recruits.

reservation (reh-ser-VEY-shun): A reservation is a piece of land set aside for a Native American tribe. Many code talkers had lived on a reservation.

runner (RUHN-er): A runner is a messenger. During wartime, a runner might deliver messages about troop movements.

translations (tranz-LAY-shunz): Translations are pieces of writing changed from one language to another language. The code talker could write translations of English messages in Navajo code.

transmit (trans-MIT): To transmit a message is to send it to a person or destination. Code talkers used radios to transmit information.

SOURCE NOTES

1-2. Robbie Christiano, Jessica King, and Shawn Tsosie. "Keith Little: Real Code Talker Interview." *Navajo Code Talkers*. Diné College and Winona State University, 2012. Web. 9 July 2015.

3. Felicia Fonseca. "Navajo Code Talker, Museum Backer Keith Little Dies." *SF Gate*. Hearst Communications, Inc., 5 January 2012. Web. 9 July 2015.

4. Franklin Fisher. "Watch Out for Foreign Agents: Authorities Say Spies Eye U.S. Troops in Hopes of Gleaning Intelligence." *www.Army.mil*. U.S. Army, 25 January 2013. Web. 10 July 2015.

5-9. Philip Johnston. "Indian Jargon Won Our Battles!" *NAU Special Collections & Archives*. Northern Arizona University, 22 June 2005. Web. 9 July 2015.

10. Tom Gorman. "Navajos Honored for War of Words." *Los Angeles Times*. Los Angeles Times Media Group, 26 July 2001. Web. 9 July 2015.

11. Emily Gust, et al. "Chester Nez: Real Code Talker Interview." *Navajo Code Talkers*. Diné College and Winona State University, 2012. Web. 9 July 2015.

12. James Hart. "Talking Code: Interview with the Real Navajo Code Talkers." *Warfare History Network*. Sovereign Media, 22 April 2014. Web. 9 July 2015.

13-14. "Navajo Code Talkers Join the Guadalcanal Battlefield." *World War II Today*. World War II Today, n.d. 9 July 2015.

15-16. Doris A. Paul. *The Navajo Code Talkers*. Pittsburgh, PA: Dorrance, 1973. Print. 32.

17. Noah Riseman. *Defending Whose Country?* Lincoln, NE: U of Nebraska P, 2012. Print. 205.

18. Ibid. 196.

19. "Navajo Code Talkers." *Arizona Stories*. PBS and Arizona State University, n.d. Web. 17 September 2015.

20. "Navajo Code Talkers and the Unbreakable Code." *CIA.gov*. The Central Intelligence Agency, 2008. Web. 9 July 2015.

21. Office of the Federal Register. *Public Papers of the Presidents of the United States: George W. Bush, 2001*. Washington, DC: Government Printing Office, 2004. Print. 917.

22. Steve Vogel. "For Navajos, an Award of Gratitude." *The Washington Post*. The Washington Post, 27 July 2001. Web. 9 July 2015.

TO LEARN MORE

Books

Blackwood, Gary. *Mysterious Messages: A History of Codes and Ciphers*. New York: Penguin, 2009.

Hunter, Sara Hoagland. *The Unbreakable Code*. New York: Cooper Square, 2007.

Tohe, Laura. *Code Talker Stories*. Tucson, AZ: Rio Nuevo, 2012.

Web Sites

Visit our Web site for links about the Navajo code talkers:

childsworld.com/links

Note to Parents, Teachers, and Librarians: We routinely verify our Web links to make sure they are safe and active sites. So encourage your readers to check them out!

INDEX